HOLBORN AND FINSBURY TRAMWAYS

Robert J Harley

MP Middleton Press

-------- FEATURES IN OTHER LONDON *TRAMWAY CLASSICS* ---------

● **Rolling Stock**

A class. LCC.	**Southwark and Deptford.**
B class. LCC/Bexley.	**Greenwich and Dartford.**
Barking cars.	**Ilford and Barking.**
Bexley cars.	**Greenwich and Dartford.**
Bluebird. LCC car 1.	**Camberwell and West Norwood.**
C class. LCC.	**Victoria and Lambeth.**
Croydon cars.	**Croydon's Tramways.**
D class. LCC.	**Wandsworth and Battersea.**
Dartford cars.	**Greenwich and Dartford.**
East Ham cars.	**East Ham and West Ham.**
Erith cars.	**Greenwich and Dartford.**
E class. LCC/LT.	**Aldgate and Stepney.**
E1 class. LCC/LT.	**Lewisham and Catford.**
E1 cars 552-601. LCC/LT.	**Hampstead and Highgate.**
E3 class. LCC/LT.	**Camberwell and West Norwood.**
E3 class. Leyton/LT.	**Walthamstow and Leyton.**
F class. LCC.	**Embankment and Waterloo.**
G class. LCC.	**Embankment and Waterloo.**
Gravesend & Northfleet cars.	**North Kent.**
H class (works). LCC/LT.	**Eltham and Woolwich.**
Horse cars. North Met./LCC.	**Aldgate and Stepney.**
HR2 class. LCC/LT.	**Camberwell and West Norwood.**

Ilford cars.	**Ilford and Barking.**
L class (works). LCC/LT.	**Holborn and Finsbury.**
Leyton cars.	**Walthamstow and Leyton.**
LT car 2.	**Wandsworth and Battersea.**
LUT car 341.	**Kingston and Wimbledon.**
M class. LCC/LT.	**Greenwich and Dartford.**
Petrol electric cars. LCC.	**Southwark and Deptford.**
SMET cars.	**Croydon's Tramways.**
T type. LUT.	**Kingston and Wimbledon.**
Walthamstow cars.	**Walthamstow and Leyton.**
West Ham cars.	**East Ham and West Ham.**

● **Miscellaneous**

Advertising on tramcars.	**Aldgate and Stepney.**
Conduit system.	**Embankment and Waterloo.**
Power supply.	**Walthamstow and Leyton.**
Request stops.	**Victoria and Lambeth.**
Section boxes.	**Eltham and Woolwich.**
Tram tours.	**Holborn and Finsbury.**

First published July 1996

ISBN 1 873793 79 0

© *Middleton Press 1996*

Design - Deborah Goodridge

Published by Middleton Press
　　　　　　　Easebourne Lane
　　　　　　　Midhurst
　　　　　　　West Sussex
　　　　　　　GU29 9AZ
　　　　　　　Tel: 01730 813169
　　　　　　　Fax: 01730 812601

Printed & bound by Biddles Ltd,
　　　　　　　Guildford and Kings Lynn

CONTENTS

Kingsway Subway and Bloomsbury   1

Holborn to Kings Cross   19

Farringdon Road   32

Rosebery Avenue to Angel, Islington   38

Smithfield   56

Aldersgate and Goswell Road   59

Clerkenwell Road and Old Street   65

Moorgate to Highbury Corner   72

Essex Road to Balls Pond Road   88

Rolling Stock - Works cars class L   103

Tram Tours   107

Finale   119

INTRODUCTION AND ACKNOWLEDGEMENTS

The two former Metropolitan Boroughs of Holborn (pronounced Hoebun) and Finsbury form the subject of this volume of Tramway Classics. Services in adjacent areas have already been described in companion books *Hampstead and Highgate Tramways*, *Aldgate and Stepney Tramways* and *Embankment and Waterloo Tramways*. Inevitably there has been some overlap in coverage, this is due to the fact that the drawing of artficial boundaries between tramways in North London is an inexact science.

Our journey into the past has been made possible by the photographers and postcard collectors whose names are recorded in the text of this book. I would particularly like to thank C.Carter for all his help with the series, also my gratitude goes to D.W.K.Jones who has supplied many rare views. Photos taken by the late Dr.Hugh Nicol have been kindly made available by his daughter Mrs S.Leitch. Views from the collection of the late Alan Watkins are by permission of Ann Watkins. London

Transport circulars and timetables have been published with the consent of the London Transport Museum, Covent Garden. Dave Jones of the LCC Tramways Trust has again excelled himself in locating views and supplying information. The archival resources of B.J."Curly" Cross have also been used, and I am very grateful for this valuable assistance. John Meredith and John Price continue to be stalwart supporters of the series and I acknowledge their help especially with the Tram Tours section. The rolling stock plan was drawn and supplied by Terry Russell. Photos by Henry Priestley and the late W.A. Camwell are from the archives of the National Tramway Museum Library which is a treasure house of historical material.

Reference books consulted include the standard works on the LCC Tramways written by E.R.Oakley, the two volume MET series by C.S.Smeeton and *North London's Tramways* by J.Barrie.

GEOGRAPHICAL SETTING

The northern approaches to the Cities of London and Westminster have formed part of the urban metropolitan landscape for over a century. Green areas such as Grays Inn and Coram's Fields are at a premium, surrounded as they are by urban housing, shops and offices. In April 1965 the Borough of Holborn was incorporated into the London Borough of Camden; Finsbury was absorbed by the London Borough of Islington.

Maps are to a scale of 1:2500; tramway junction maps drawn by the late F.Merton Atkins have also been used to augment the text.

HISTORICAL BACKGROUND

The region covered by this book was originally administered by Middlesex until the formation of the London County Council in 1889. Before this transfer took place, horse tramways operated by the North Metropolitan Company had opened in July 1871 from Islington Green to the City boundary at Ropemaker Street, Finsbury. Further lines followed in 1872 from City Road to Shoreditch, and from Islington Green to Dalston Junction via Essex Road. In the following year horse drawn trams appeared along Old Street and on Goswell Road from Angel, Islington to Aldersgate; City Road to Balls Pond Road via Southgate Road and Bridport Place opened in May 1874. Canonbury Road and New North Road were connected to the system in March 1879. Another tramway operator, the London Street Tramways Company, inaugurated services along Farringdon Road in 1885 and Grays Inn Road in 1889.

In May 1895 the following North Metropolitan horse car services were operating:

Archway Tavern to Moorgate via Liverpool Road....White
Archway Tavern to Moorgate via Upper Street....Blue
Finsbury Park to Moorgate via Upper Street....Yellow
Finsbury Park to Moorgate via Canonbury....Brown
Poplar to Bloomsbury....Brown
Stamford Hill to Holborn....Green
Stamford Hill to Moorgate....Red
Hackney to Aldersgate....Green
Lea Bridge Road to Bloomsbury....Yellow and Blue
Manor House to Moorgate....Green

Note that in those days of restricted literacy, each service was allocated cars painted in a different livery to help passengers identify the service they required.

The London Street Tramways operated the following services:

Hampstead to Holborn
Highgate Road to Holborn
Caledonian Road to Holborn
Caledonian Road to Clerkenwell

From the 1890s onwards the writing was on the wall as far as the horse tramway companies were concerned; the LCC began to acquire cars and lines with a view to conversion to electric operation based on the underground conduit system of current collection. This method was more expensive than the conventional overhead wire means of supplying electricity to the vehicles, however, progress began in earnest in the first decade of the twentieth century. The first section of the Kingsway Subway opened in February 1906 with single deck cars working from Angel, Islington via Rosebery Avenue and Theobalds Road to Aldwych Station. Reconstruction of the former horse tramways then gained momentum. In 1907 electric lines opened in Clerkenwell Road, Old Street, Goswell Road, Grays Inn Road and City Road. In 1908 St John Street was electrified and in the next year tracks in Kings Cross Road, Swinton Street and Essex Road were added to the network. Kings Cross Bridge and Baring Street to Balls Pond Road via Southgate Road opened in 1912 to be followed by Balls Pond Road junction and Dorset Street in 1913. Finally in June 1914 the section opened from Highbury Station to City Road via New North Road.

The LCC trams in their purple lake and primrose livery soon became a familiar feature of street life in this area; they offered a reliable and frequent service backed up by cheap fares. The municipal cars were soon joined by vehicles belonging to the Metropolitan Electric Tramways which operated joint services to various inner London termini. On 1st March 1913 service 59 commenced from Edmonton Town Hall to Holborn; on 23rd June MET cars appeared on service 79, Smithfield to Waltham Cross. Holborn was joined to North Finchley

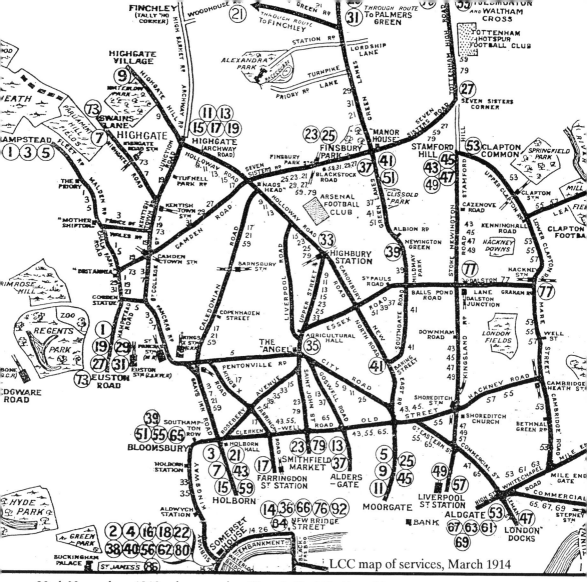

LCC map of services, March 1914

on 23rd November 1913 when service 21 started running, this was followed the next year by service 51, Muswell Hill to Bloomsbury, which commenced operation on 15th August, just after the declaration of war.

During wartime it became imperative that the capital's transport system work at full efficiency and to further this aim LCC service 9 was extended to Barnet on 24th September 1914. After the demands of the First World War had been successfully met, the local tramways settled down to a period of stability and they more than held their own against a clutch of competing bus companies.

Services operating in November 1928:

3 Hampstead to Holborn
5 Hampstead to Moorgate
7 Parliament Hill Fields to Holborn
9 North Finchley to Moorgate
11 Highgate Village to Moorgate
13 Highgate to Aldersgate
15 Parliament Hill Fields to Moorgate
17 Highgate to Farringdon Street Station
21 North Finchley to Holborn
35 Highgate to Elephant & Castle - via Kingsway Subway
37 Manor House to Aldersgate
39 Bruce Grove to Aldersgate
41 Manor House to Moorgate
43 Stamford Hill to Holborn
45 Stamford Hill to Moorgate
51 Muswell Hill to Bloomsbury
55 Leyton Station to Bloomsbury
59 Edmonton to Holborn
65 Blackwall Tunnel to Bloomsbury
75 Stamford Hill to Holborn
77 West India Docks to Aldersgate
79 Waltham Cross to Smithfield
81 Epping Forest to Bloomsbury
83 Stamford Hill to Moorgate

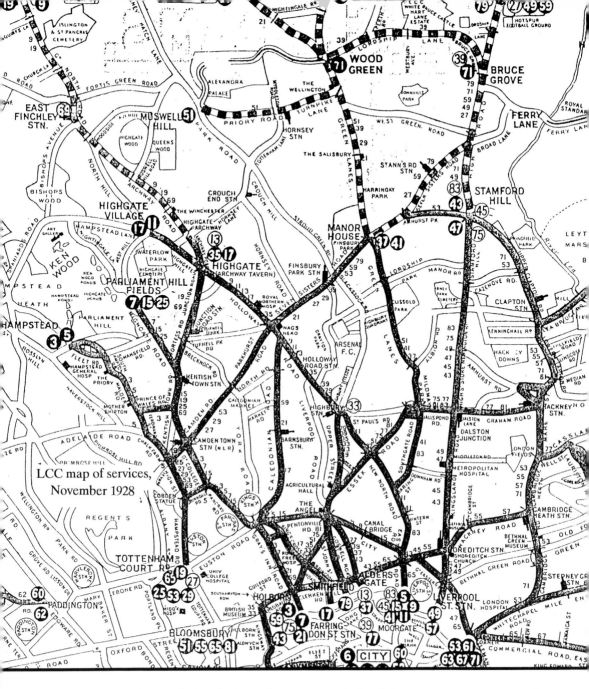

LCC map of services, November 1928

A major project carried out in the early 1930s was the enlargement of the Kingsway Subway for double deck operation and from 15th January 1931 new services 31, 33 and 35 provided vital north-south links in the tramway system. However, the coming of the London Passenger Transport Board in July 1933 put paid to any further tramway expansion in the capital and the new owners were soon formulating plans to introduce trolleybuses in place of tramcars. One by one the old, familiar tram services disappeared and after the 65 was converted in June 1940 only the three Kingsway Subway services remained. They soldiered on throughout the Second World War, thus outliving all other North London tramways by some years. This tramway Indian summer lasted until 5th April 1952 when services 33 and 35 were replaced by diesel buses. Car 185 was the last passenger tram through the subway and this wonderful piece of transport engineering was then closed. The replacing buses were rerouted to add to the congestion in neighbouring streets.

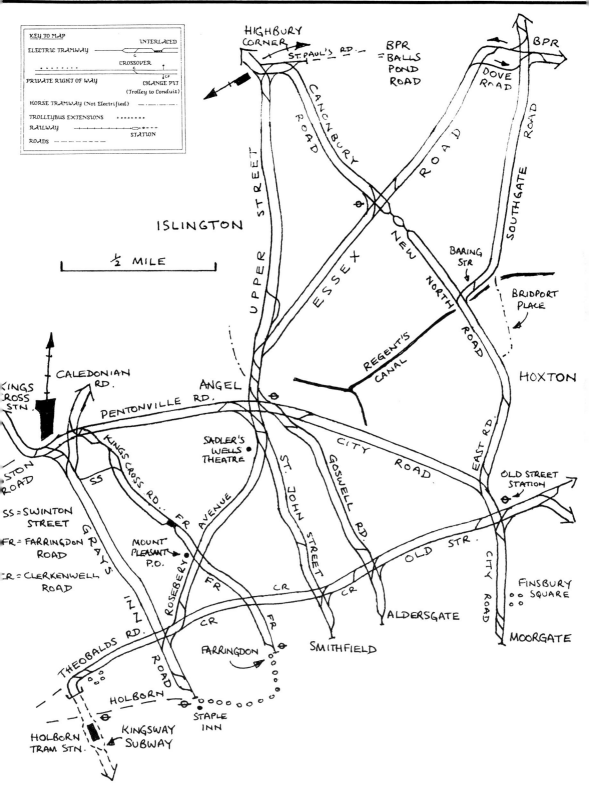

KINGSWAY SUBWAY AND BLOOMSBURY

1. Out of the past a vision of the future - such was the Kingsway Subway. This sub-surface tramway was years ahead of its time when the final section from Aldwych Station to the Embankment opened on 10th April 1908. This view dates from double deck days and features a crossover south of Holborn Station. (D.W.K.Jones)

2. Bloomsbury beckons as we gaze up the 1 in 10 (10%) ramp which leads to Southampton Row. You can almost hear the sound of the traction motors echoing from the walls as this tram makes its descent. In the shadows to the left of the picture an inspector keeps a wary eye on the photographer. (D.W.K.Jones)

3.   In this scene from the early 1930s the motorman of car 1936 has to exercise great skill and caution as he advances slowly on the wet rails at the entrance to the subway. Note that southbound road traffic is passing both sides of the subway. Further views at this location are included in companion volume *Embankment and Waterloo Tramways*.
(G.N.Southerden)

4.   In this rare overhead view we note an E3 class car on service 35 about to turn into Theobalds Road. A duty inspector stands on the Embankment bound track. On more than one occasion the presence of this official has deterred an errant motorist attempting to use the subway as a short cut.   (D.W.K.Jones)

5. This is the first of three views which shows the loading island in Theobalds Road from contrasting angles. Here we are looking east past a stationary 33 tram. (A.J.Watkins)

6. From above we observe an orderly queue waiting to board a southbound car. The detail of the trolley poles on the tram's roof will be noted by many tramway modellers who strive to achieve perfection in miniature. (D.W.K.Jones)

7. We now position ourselves at ground level at a point protected by temporary roadworks. The points on the facing crossover are set, as one might expect, for the subway. This view was taken on 5th April 1952, the last day of operation. The entrance to the subway and the ramp complete with conduit tracks all survive in 1996. (J.C.Gillham)

8. A 33 sets off along Theobalds Road on the next leg of its North London journey to Manor House. On the right of this photo can be seen the trolleybus wiring which enters Parton Street and forms part of the loop terminus installed here in 1939. (D.W.K.Jones)

9. The sign - BOMBED SITE CAR PARK - to the right of car 1916 gives a clue to the devastation which was visited on this area during the war. We also catch a rather rural glimpse of trees in Red Lion Square which are framed by a trolleybus traction standard. (D.Jones Coll.)

10. The same location as the previous photo, but the clock has now been turned back to just before the war - before the disappearance of many of the properties hereabouts. At this time trams operating services 31, 33 and 35 were allocated in strict sequence to various depots. Cars 1904-1921 were shedded at Hackney, cars 1922-1951 at Holloway, cars 1952-1968 at Wandsworth, cars 1969-1988 at Camberwell and cars 1989-2003 at Norwood. (H.B.Priestley)

11. A standard LCC E1 car in brown and cream livery pauses at Bloomsbury before returning to Leyton on service 81. Regulations stated that only metal bodied trams were allowed in the subway, thus this E1 car whose bodywork was mainly wooden was not permitted to proceed further. In any case in this 1928 view the descent from Southampton Row would have lopped off the top deck as the subway was originally constructed for single deckers only! (F.Grunwald)

12. The crew of car 654 pose for a photograph shortly after this vehicle, which was a member of the second batch of class E cars, was delivered in 1907. Conditions for the motorman could be harsh especially when the elements were against him and icy wind and rain blew across the open driving platform. The Metropolitan Police, who were the licensing authority, adopted a very old fashioned attitude to windscreen protection for motormen and the capital had to wait well into the 1930s before all enclosed cars were the norm. (D.Jones Coll.)

ROUTE No. 15.

Highbury Station to Tooley-street (Bermondsey-street), "Angel" to Vauxhall, and St. Paul's-road to Southampton-row (Electric Traction).

1. Union Chapel.
2. Islington Church.
3. Collins' Music Hall.
4. Palace Theatre.
5. Royal Agricultural Hall.
6. New Islington Empire.
7. Sadler's Wells Theatre.
8. Parcel Post Office.
9. Gray's Inn.
10. Central School of Arts and Crafts.
11. London Day Training School.
12. Kingsway Theatre.
13. Whitney Theatre.
14. Strand Theatre (late Waldorf Theatre).
15. Gaiety Theatre.
16. Royal Courts of Justice.
17. Somerset House.

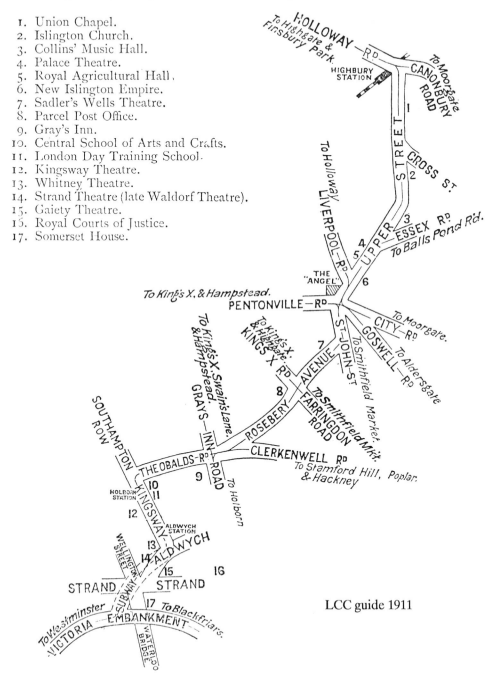

LCC guide 1911

13. Caught in a downpour at Bloomsbury, car 1964 edges forward in company with a General motor bus. Service 31 provided a useful link betwen Hackney in the east and Battersea in the south-west. In its final form before bus replacement in September 1950, it ran from Wandsworth to Islington Green. (G.N.Southerden)

14. Car 1107 has just run forward over the facing crossover. An inspector stops the traffic for passengers to alight whilst the next load of customers boards. Trade was brisk in those days! The fare from Bloomsbury to East Ham Town Hall was a mere sixpence (2p). (C.F.Klapper)

15. The motorman of the oncoming ex West Ham car puts his arm out to warn other road users as he guides his charge on to the facing crossover. The points are being switched by the pointsman standing near the kerb outside the Imperial Milk Bar. (H.B.Priestley)

16. This picture presents an interesting contrast with the previous view. The street corner to the right of car 1993 has been a victim of the "blitz" and awaits redevelopment. In the distance Theobalds Road crosses Grays Inn Road and a tram can just be seen at the foot of Rosebery Avenue. (R.B.Parr/NTM)

17. One final look at Bloomsbury terminus reveals the pointsman at his post; car 891 waits to cross to the eastbound track. This is the last week of service 81 which succumbed to the trolleybus on 11th June 1939. (D.Jones Coll.)

18. Continuing the theme of last tram days, we encounter car 176 rolling sedately along Theobalds Road. On the dash is chalked the message - GOOD-BYE OLD PAL. (C.Carter)

19. MET cars seem to want to take possession of Holborn terminus. What a difference in body styles between Feltham type car 344 and MET type H car 291! The more modern vehicle was delivered in 1931 and it seems to have overshot the points somewhat. Car 344 will have to back up a little to let car 291 out of the terminal stub. (G.N.Southerden)

21. We look north along Grays Inn Road past the LCC car on Service 75, the MET Feltham on service 21 and another older MET vehicle on service 59. (G.N.Southerden)

20. Time marches on - it is now 3.45 pm on 26th June 1937 and we observe car 2171 in London Transport red and cream livery; this tram was formerly MET type H car 239. In the background Staple Inn is being restored. The building was originally a hostelry where wool was weighed and taxed; it dates from 1586 and its most famous inhabitant was Dr.Johnson who moved there in March 1759. Unfortunately the restored structure was devastated in 1944 by a flying bomb. The inn received a complete rebuild in 1953-54. (H.Nicol)

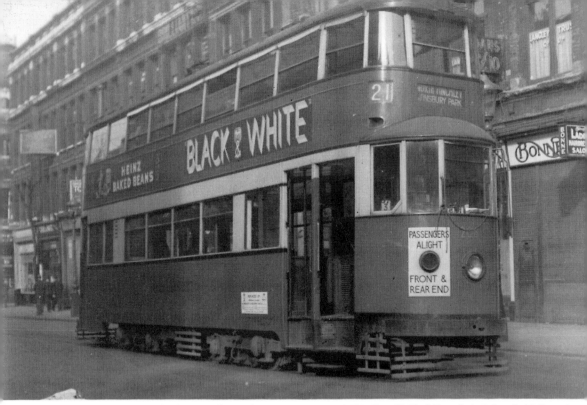

22. The next arrival at Holborn has a very distinctive pedigree. This car first emerged as MET car 341, and on acquisition by LT it was renumbered 2085. Finally it assumed the guise of Leeds 526 after the Felthams were sold in 1949/50. Car 526 left Leeds in March 1960 and was shipped to Boston. It now resides at the Seashore Trolley Museum, Kennebunkport, Maine. (B.J.Cross Coll.)

Grays Inn/Holborn Hall 1916

23. Car 2218 was formerly MET type H car 286; it was withdrawn in May 1938. Service 59 lasted a little longer, perishing on 16th October 1938. (D.Jones Coll.)

24. A fine, summer's day lifts the spirits of Londoners. The red and cream paintwork of car 1056 gleams in the sunshine as a gentle breeze ruffles the leaves in Grays Inn Road. This idyllic scene will not last many months longer as trolleybus overhead is already in place and service 43 will be delivered the "coup de grace" on 5th February 1939.

(H.B.Priestley)

25. Car 635 passes a traffic island at the northern end of Grays Inn Road, by Derby Street. Note that this tram has but a single trolley pole, this is rather redundant because service 7 ran wholly over conduit tracks. (R.J.Harley Coll.)

26. The haze has now cleared to reveal MET car 245 with a triangular warning sign on its dash to remind motorists to keep a safe distance when braking. The 1920s pedestrian refuge seems a lot more substantial than the plastic traffic bollards of the 1990s. (B.J.Cross Coll.)

27. This view was taken on 2nd March 1938 and the location is at the junction of tracks leading from Grays Inn Road into Caledonian Road. The transition period from tram to trolleybus is well under way and one of the new vehicles comes up behind car 2174 which will be withdrawn in November.
(G.Freeze/NTM)

28. We move over to the citybound track to observe car 2185 in LT livery, but retaining its cream painted stair stringer. This vehicle has obviously not been posted to Charlton Works by the new regime, since cars sent to the ex-LCC Central Repair Depot at Charlton would normally receive an LT red painted staircase.
(A.J.Watkins Coll.)

29. The heyday of London's tramways is apparent at Kings Cross where no motorized competition is on hand to challenge the trams' supremacy. Car 281 will have to get a move on as an impatient Feltham is snapping at its heels. Further photos of the Kings Cross area are included in *Hampstead and Highgate Tramways*. (C.Carter)

Kings Cross 1916

30. The Felthams represented a complete break with tradition. They transformed the metropolitan tramway scene, and for sheer class and luxury they have never been matched on the streets of London. Car 335 glides into the picture with the motorman concentrating on the car in front which he will follow along Grays Inn Road to Holborn terminus. (G.N.Southerden)

31. In the foreground the tramlines from Grays Inn Road join those used by services from Pentonville Road and Kings Cross Road. Kings Cross station is on the right and St.Pancras station is in the background. In the foreground is an E class car which possesses a trolley plank but no trolley pole. A full description of this class of tram can be found in *Aldgate and Stepney Tramways*. (R.J.Harley Coll.)

32. The Farringdon terminus was at the corner of Cowcross Street near Farringdon Street station. The replacing trolleybuses were extended across Holborn Circus to form a loop with the Grays Inn Road routes. Car 638 works out its last days on service 17 before abandonment on 6th March 1938. (W.A.Camwell)

33. An ex-Walthamstow car is spotted by the camera on Farringdon Road not long after the formation of LT in 1933. These particular cars were renowned for generating all sorts of gear and motor noises; you could tell when an ex-Walthamstow was approaching! On the credit side, when the driver notched up, all the competition was left standing, and in the hands of an "enthusiastic" motorman one of these trams could easily break the 30 mph speed limit. (D.Jones Coll.)

Extract from LT timetable, December 1935.

		MON. to FRI.		SATURDAY		SUNDAY	
		First	Last	First	Last	First	Last
7 HIGHGATE — KINGS X — FARRINGDON ST., Via Holloway, Caledonian Rd., Kings X., Farringdon Rd Service Interval, 2—8 mins. Journey time, 26 mins. Through fare 3d. Extended to E. Finchley wkdy. rush hrs.	Highgate (Archway Tav.) to Farringdon St.	5 30	5 54	11 44	5 30	5 54	12 0	7 15	12 8
	Farringdon St. Stn. to Highgate (Archway Tav)	6 2	6 22	12 13	6 2	6 22	12 25	7 40	12 32
	East Finchley to Farringdon Street..........	7 7	7 12	6 44	7 7	7 12	2 43	......	....
	Farringdon St. Stn. to East Finchley........	6 40	6 56	7 2	6 40	6 56	2 9	......	....

34. A somewhat slower, but no less interesting service 17 tram is M class car 1452 which dates from 1910 and was allocated to the Highgate Hill line. This view dates from before June 1929 when car 1452 was temporarily withdrawn to be upgraded in the LCC's "Pullmanisation" programme. (H.Nicol)

35. There appears to be a mad dash to catch car 1059 before it leaves the terminus. Perhaps several of these folk have transferred from the nearby Farringdon Street station. This station was opened by the Metropolitan Railway in 1863 and the underground lines were electrified in 1905. (C.F.Klapper)

36. A last look at Farringdon terminus shows car 831 about to depart. In a few days time the motorman will be able to exchange his open driving platform for a seat in an all enclosed trolleybus on route 617. (C.F.Klapper)

37. Near Calthorpe Street there was an interesting section of interlaced track. One can only assume this layout was adopted because it wasn't worth installing two sets of points. It lasted until tramway abandonment along Farringdon Road.   (D.Jones Coll.)

Extract from LT timetable, December 1935.

NOTE : For all-night services, see pages 192-193.

		MON. to FRI.		SATURDAY		SUNDAY	
		First	Last	First	Last	First	Last
35 **FOREST HILL — EMBANKMENT — HIGHGATE**	Forest Hill Stn. to Camberwell Green........	6 33	6 39	12 51	6 33	6 39	12 54	6 25	12 ?
Via Brockley Rise, Crofton Park, Brockley Stn., New Cross	Forest Hill Stn. to Highgate (Archway Tavern)	6 33	6 39	12 14	6 33	6 39	11 38	6 25	12
Peckham, Camberwell Green, Elephant, Westminster Bge.	Forest Hill Stn. to Bloomsbury..............	6 33	6 39	12 14	6 33	6 39	11 44	6 25	12
Embankment, KINGSWAY SUBWAY, Bloomsbury, Angel,	Highgate (Archway Tav.) to Forest Hill Stn.	5 48	5 54	11 25	5 48	5 54	11 27	5 34	11
Upper Street, Highbury, Holloway.	Highgate (Archway Tav.) to New Cross....	5 48	5 54	11 40	5 48	5 54	11 45	5 34	12
Service interval, 6—10 mins. Journey time 85 mins.	Highgate (Archway Tav.) to Camberwell Gn.	5 48	5 54	12 22	5 48	5 54	12 33	5 34	12
Certain cars operate Elephant and Castle—Highbury Stn.	Highgate (Archway Tav.) to Westminster...	4 44	4 56	12 22	4 44	4 56	12 33	5 34	12
only, Mon. to Fri., slack hours. Through fare, 9d., Forest	Westminster to Highgate (Archway Tav.) ..	5 18	5 36	1	2	5 18	5 36	12 52	6 20	12
Hill — Southampton Row 5d., Southampton Row —	Camberwell Green to Highgate (Archway Tav.)	6 12	6 21	12 44	6 12	6 21	12* 9	6 5	12
Highgate 4d.	* Later cars until 12.42 to Holloway (Nags Head)								

38. The date is 5th August 1929 and we leave our 17 tram in Farringdon Road and cross over to Rosebery Avenue where a service 35 single decker awaits. A group of lads all attired in their "Sunday best" seems to be making a meal of leaving car 563. The passengers who are sandwiched together on longitudinal bench seats will have to be a little more patient before the conductor signals the right of way to cross the Farringdon Road metals.
(G.N.Southerden)

39. Another visitor to Rosebery Avenue is MET car 171, a rather antique looking type D tramcar built in 1906. These vehicles were modified with conduit collection gear so that they could participate on joint services with the LCC. They continued to work on service 51 until 1931 when they were sent for scrap.
(G.N.Southerden)

ROUTE No. 6.

Moorgate and Smithfield Market to Finsbury Park; Holborn, Aldersgate and Moorgate to Highgate; Moorgate to Highgate Village (Electric Traction); and Liverpool Road (Horse Traction).

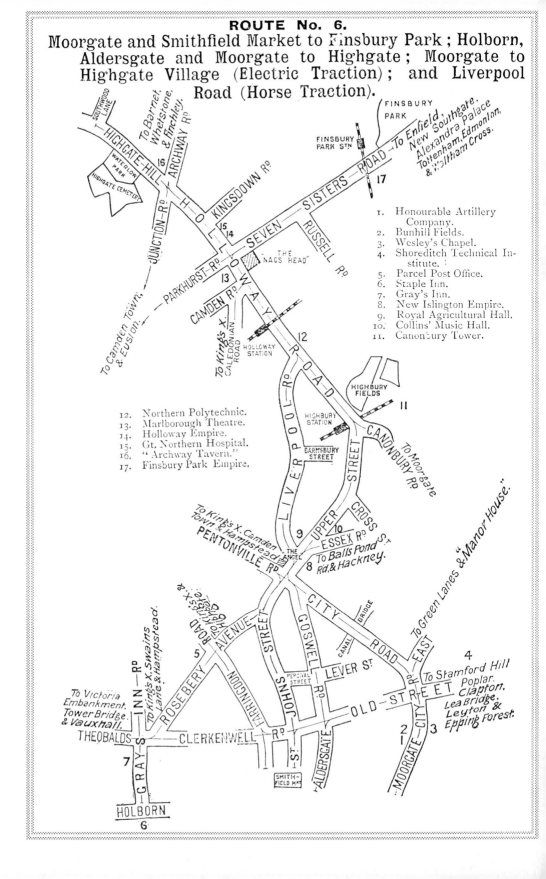

1. Honourable Artillery Company.
2. Bunhill Fields.
3. Wesley's Chapel.
4. Shoreditch Technical Institute.
5. Parcel Post Office.
6. Staple Inn.
7. Gray's Inn.
8. New Islington Empire.
9. Royal Agricultural Hall.
10. Collins' Music Hall.
11. Canonbury Tower.

12. Northern Polytechnic.
13. Marlborough Theatre.
14. Holloway Empire.
15. Gt. Northern Hospital.
16. "Archway Tavern."
17. Finsbury Park Empire.

40. A similar view to the previous picture but now we are in the early 1950s and the large Mount Pleasant sorting office has been erected on the corner of Rosebery Avenue and Farringdon Road. This vast complex was completed in 1934 and is served by the Post Office Railway. Electrically driven parcels and mail trains run underground to Whitechapel, Liverpool Street Station and Paddington. (C.Carter)

41. The former crossing with service 17 has now been lifted and replaced with straight track for services 31, 33 and 35. Car 178 is an ex-Leyton vehicle which is working to West Norwood via the Kingsway Subway. This class of car is extensively described in *Walthamstow and Leyton Tramways*. (B.J.Cross Coll.)

42. In an age when the tram represented the only mechanized form of transport in Rosebery Avenue, the single deck car heading towards Aldwych can easily outpace its horse drawn rivals. This picture was taken shortly after the first section of the Kingsway Subway was opened and it probably dates from the summer of 1906. (J.H.Price Coll.)

43. When all else fails and the traffic in the area slithers to a halt, you could always rely on the trams to get you home. At least that was the case on 29th March 1952 when a late snowfall caused chaos in Central London. Wouldn't it be nice if this efficient transport system were still around to cope with the vagaries of the British weather? (J.C.Gillham)

44. Car 554 passes Finsbury Town Hall. The three lights below the indicator were illuminated at night as an indication of the car's route. The service from Highbury Station to Tower Bridge via the Kingsway Subway would have shown a RED-GREEN-RED combination. (J.H.Price Coll.)

45. Patrons can arrive in style at Sadler's Wells Theatre. This establishment was rebuilt in 1931 and it takes its name from a mineral water spring which was brought to public attention in 1683 by a Mr Sadler. (D.Jones Coll.)

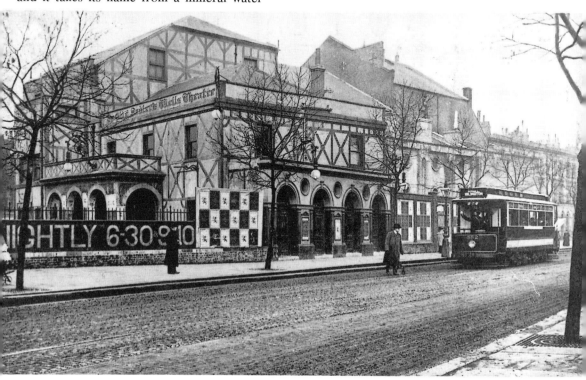

46. Tram leads trolleybus at the parting of the ways between Rosebery Avenue and St.John Street. The latter thoroughfare was last used by trams in October 1938 when service 79 ceased. (F.W.Ivey/LTPS)

47. Our line of sight stretches past car 1995 along St.John Street to the Angel, Islington. On the extreme left of the picture is a section box and telephone. These vital pieces of equipment are described in *Eltham and Woolwich Tramways*. (B.J.Cross Coll.)

48. If proof were needed that this locality is not all close packed houses, then this view of Myddelton Square off St.John Street should demonstrate that there existed some degree of urban elegance midst the metropolitan gloom. Tramlines in the foreground await the introduction of the electric cars.
(J.H.Price Coll.)

49. Electric traction is well in evidence on the approach to the Angel from St.John Street. A short way after passing the traffic lights the two trams shown here will go their separate ways to Manor House (33) and Highgate (35) respectively. (C.Carter)

50. A much older view than the previous photograph shows car 558 on one of its first runs over the new electric tramway. It is early in 1906 and the horse bus driver must be feeling the chill of competition coupled with the fear of seeing his passengers desert to the modern LCC vehicle. (J.H.Price Coll.)

51. As the trolleybus conversion of North London took its toll of the remaining tramways, so the track layout at the Angel was simplified. In this view dated 4th November 1948 the roadway is still sett paved, but the points and crossings of previous years have largely disappeared. Note the PW department's wooden hut and the red and white TRACK UP signs. (A.J.Watkins)

52. The Angel tube station opened on 17th November 1901 as part of the City & South London Railway Company's electric line. Electric trams were later on the scene and City Road first witnessed LCC conduit equipped cars in July 1907. In this picture, taken towards the end of the tramway era in City Road, we observe car 521 on its way to Moorgate. (A.J.Watkins Coll.)

53. We look west from the City Road/Goswell Road junction towards Pentonville Road. A lone horse car crosses into Islington High Street as car 873 waits to proceed in the direction of Kings Cross. (R.J.Harley Coll.)

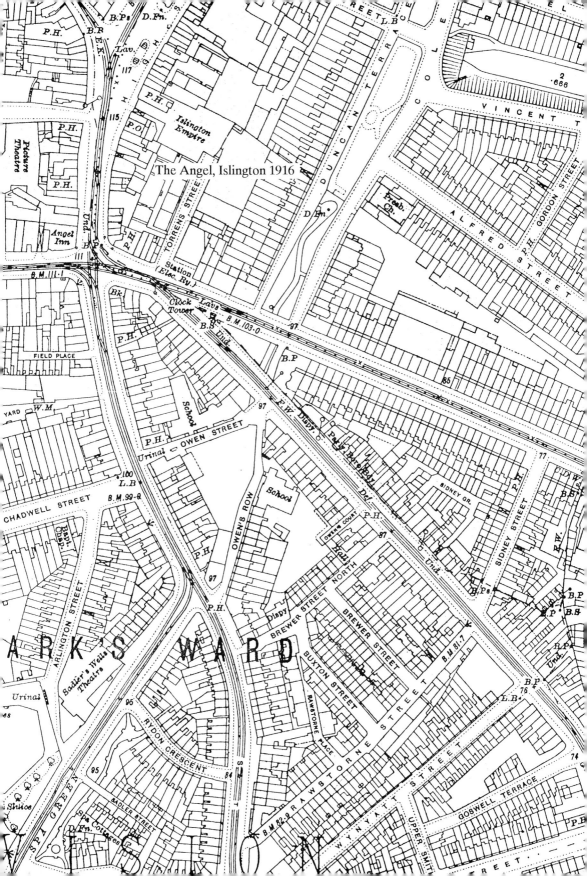

The Angel, Islington 1916

54. The conductor of car 1005 glances over to the LCC inspector who is no doubt scribbling a note about some minor time-keeping misdemeanour. One hopes the poor conductor won't get "carpetted" when he goes off shift. In those days a conductor worked a sixty hour week for a wage of 28/6 to 37/6 (£1.42 to £1.87); the inspector did marginally better at 42/- (£2.10) per week! (D.Jones Coll.)

55. Car 1, the LCC's answer to the MET Felthams, has halted on its progress southwards to let a couple of 77s get out of the way. The General motor bus bears an advert with medicinal claims which would not pass muster with the present day Advertising Standards Authority! (G.N.Southerden)

SMITHFIELD

56. On 3rd July 1938 car 2169, ex-MET type H car 237, stands at the end of the track in St.John Street near Smithfield Market. A turning circle for the replacing trolleybuses is already in place. Trolleybus route 679 lasted until 25th April 1961 and now only diesel fumes waft around here. (W.A.Camwell)

ROUTE 5.

Holborn to Finsbury Park; Farringdon-street Station to Highgate (Electric Traction).

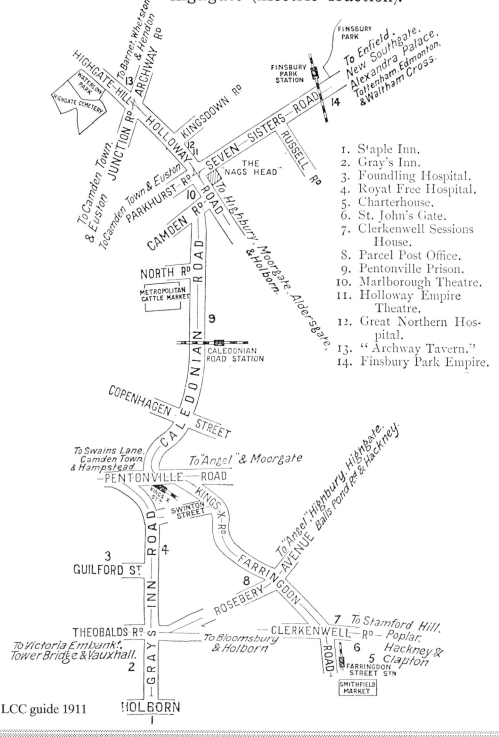

1. Staple Inn.
2. Gray's Inn.
3. Foundling Hospital.
4. Royal Free Hospital.
5. Charterhouse.
6. St. John's Gate.
7. Clerkenwell Sessions House.
8. Parcel Post Office.
9. Pentonville Prison.
10. Marlborough Theatre.
11. Holloway Empire Theatre.
12. Great Northern Hospital.
13. "Archway Tavern."
14. Finsbury Park Empire.

LCC guide 1911

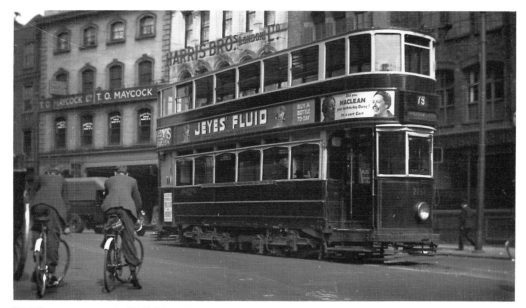

57. The tramway at Smithfield ended just short of the City of London boundary. Passengers from this tram would have had to walk, take a bus or go by tube to complete their journey. However, the City Fathers were totally consistent in their treatment of supposed "working class" vehicles and the trolleybuses got almost the same nonsensical treatment. (D.Jones Coll.)

58. Car 2271 is still in splendid condition and looks all the world as if it could complete another thirty years of service. This tram was formerly MET type G car 226 which first saw the light of day in 1909 as an open top tram. It was fitted with a plough carrier in 1912/15 and achieved top covered status in the 1928-30 modernisation programme. Windscreens were added in 1931 and the car was finally scrapped at the end of 1938. (H.B.Priestley)

ALDERSGATE AND
GOSWELL ROAD

59. After a walk across Charterhouse Square
we find ourselves at Aldersgate. On 3rd July
1938 car 890 occupies the terminal stub. The
rails in this case ended exactly where the City
of London began, so precise was the legal
measurement! (W.A.Camwell)

60. The terminus was situated opposite Fann Street. Car 601, depicted here taking on passengers, survived the war to finish up in Abbey Wood Depot during the final days of the system. Did the driver of Abbey Mills Papers van ELR 150 have to brake suddenly for the couple emerging from the other end of the tram? (H.B.Priestley)

Extract from LT timetable, December 1935.

	MON. to FRI.		SATURDAY		SUNDAY	
	First	Last	First	Last	First	Last
West India Docks to Aldersgate............	4 52	5 18	1030	4 52	5 18	1121	8 12	1125	......
West India Docks to Angel Islington......	4 52	5 18	1050	4 52	5 18	1121	8 12	1125	......
West India Docks to Hackney Station......	4 52	5 18	12 7	4 52	5 18	1247	7 44	1255	......
Aldersgate to West India Docks.............	4 2	5 2	1119	4 2	5 2	12 0	9 2	1210	......
Aldersgate to Hackney Station..............	4 2	5 2	1119	4 2	5 2	12 6	9 2	1210	......
Hackney Stn. to West India Docks..........	4 23	4 54	1143	4 23	4 54	1222	7 21	1232	......
Hackney Stn. to Aldersgate................	3 30	4 28	1052	3 30	4 28	1143	8 34	1147	......
Angel, Islington to Hackney Stn..............	4 6	5 7	1131	4 6	5 7	12 9	9 5	1213	......

7 WEST INDIA DOCKS — ALDERSGATE
Via Burdett Rd., Mile End, Victoria Pk., Hackney, Dalston, Essex Rd., Angel, Goswell Road. Through fare 5d. Service Interval, 4–8 mins. Journey time, 46 mins. Additional cars operate West India Docks—Southgate Road on Sundays, Service interval 3 mins.

ROUTE No. 10.

Aldersgate to Mare Street, Hackney (Horse and Electric Traction).

1. Charterhouse.

2. New Islington Empire.

3. Royal Agricultural Hall.

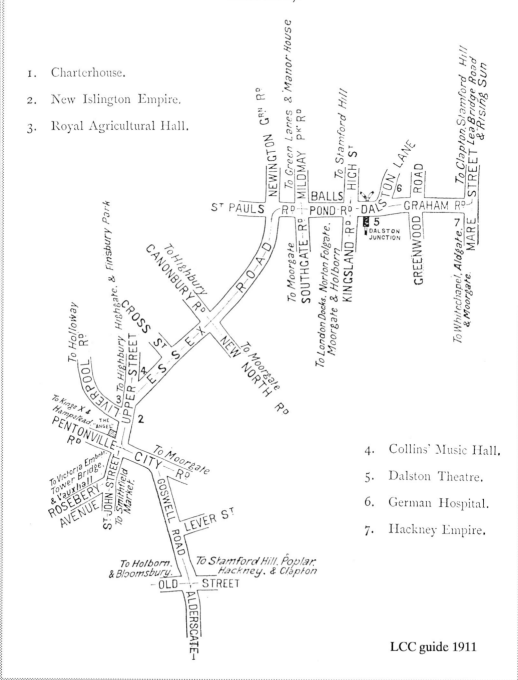

4. Collins' Music Hall.

5. Dalston Theatre.

6. German Hospital.

7. Hackney Empire.

LCC guide 1911

61. As in picture 57 this tram carries the message of an advertising campaign which features contemporary "variety" and radio stars to extoll the virtues Maclean's Toothpaste. However, there seems to be nobody about on this occasion to take note of Reginald Foort's exhortations! (D.A.Thompson)

62. Car 575 is at the corner of Goswell Road and Clerkenwell Road. When the lights change, it will resume its course past the Hat and Feathers public house. This southern part of Goswell Road to Aldersgate was never converted to trolleybuses. (H.B.Priestley)

63. At the northern end of Goswell Road by the Angel tube station service 77 cars met other trams travelling along City Road. As he approaches the junction, the motorman of car 1203 remains alert just in case the tram on the extreme left tries to slip in front of him. (H.B.Priestley)

64. We have now come full circle from picture 52, and we are back at the Angel. MET car 225 provides a useful connection from Aldersgate to Muswell Hill on service 51. On arrival at the terminus passengers could change to a single deck MET car for the ride up to Alexandra Palace. Thus for a few pennies an inner city family could enjoy a breath of fresh air and a picnic in the park. (H.Nicol)

CLERKENWELL ROAD AND OLD STREET

65. Clerkenwell Road by St.John's Square on 26th July 1938 - car 1305 in newly repainted condition joins the traffic queue waiting to cross the St.John Street junction. Note the splendid BSA motorcycle on the right of the picture. (H.B.Priestley)

Extract from LT timetable, December 1935.

	MON. to FRI.		SATURDAY		SUNDAY	
	First	Last	First	Last	First	Last
POPLAR (Blackwall Tunnel) — BLOOMSBURY* Via Commercial Rd. Commercial St. Old St. Clerkenwell Road. Extended to East Ham Town Hall Weekday Rush Hours, and to Barking Broadway Saturdays p.m Service Interval Bloomsbury—E. Ham Town Hall 2-3 mins. E. Ham, Town Hall—Barking, 4 mins. Journey time, Bloomsbury—Blackwall Tun. 32 mins.— E. Ham Town Hall 51 mins.,—Barking Bdy. 57 mins. Through fare 6d. * CERTAIN CARS OPERATE TO & FROM SMITHFIELD MARKET, WEEKDAY RUSH HOURS.						
Poplar (Blackwall Tunnel) to Bloomsbury..	4 26	5 1130	4 26	5 12 4	4 51	5 4 1144
Canning Town (Iron Bridge) to Bloomsbury	4 23	5 28 54	4 23	5 2 12 2	......	......
Canning Town (Fire Station) to Bloomsbury	5 56	6 28 52	5 56	6 2 12 0	......	......
East Ham Town Hall to Bloomsbury, morning	6 50	6 56 8 29	6 50	6 56 8 29	......	......
" " " " afternoon	4 48	4 51 8 38	1231	1234 11 14	......	......
Bloomsbury to Canning Town Fire Station....	5 43	5 547 41	5 43	5 53 11 56	......	......
Bloomsbury to Poplar (Aberfeldy St.)........	5 8	5 43 12 6	5 8	5 43 12 40	5 27	5 40 1216
Bloomsbury to East Ham Town Hall, morning	6 14	6 20 7 22	5 53	5 59 7 22	......	......
" " " " afternoon	3 44	3 47 7 41	1128	1132 10 4	......	......
Bloomsbury to Barking......................	......	......	1 6	1 14 10 4	......	......
Barking to Bloomsbury.....................	......	......	2 1	2 5 11 9	......	......
All-night service, Poplar—Bloomsbury.						

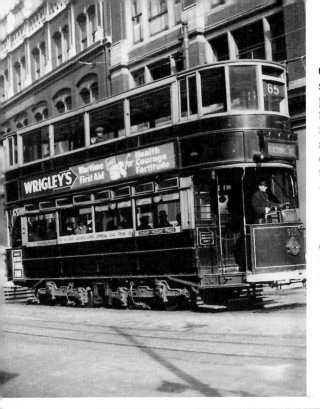

66. Wartime blackout regulations have caused some of the changes of appearance in this photo. Car 923 now sports white painted fenders and a headlamp mask. Inspite of the national emergency the tramway replacement scheme continues and service 65 will have the dubious distinction of being part of the last tram to trolleybus conversion on 9th June 1940. (D.Jones Coll.)

67. For those students of conduit pointwork this is a fine study of a trailing crossover. Also evident in this view are the metal hatch covers by the conduit slot, these could be raised to release a trapped plough or to inspect the current collecting T rails. A full account of the conduit system appears in *Embankment and Waterloo Tramways*. Looking up from the rails, we observe a short working car on service 65 and a tram on service 31 further down the track. (H.B.Priestley)

68. We now arrive at the corner of Old Street and City Road. Was the motorist a former motorman for whom old railbound habits died hard? Whatever the truth of the matter, it seems a strange place to hide, sandwiched between the fenders of two weighty tramcars. (H.B.Priestley)

		MON. to FRI.		**SATURDAY**		**SUNDAY**	
		First	Last	First	Last	First	Last
STAMFORD HILL — DALSTON — HOLBORN	Stamford Hill to Holborn....................						
Via Stoke Newington, Kingsland Rd., Shoreditch,	Holborn to Stamford Hill....................	4 12	4 20	12 10	4 12	4 20	12 20	4 15	12 20	......
Service int. 4–10 mins. Journey time, 33 mins. Fare 4d.	All-night service, Stamford Hill-Holborn	4 48	4 56	12 43	4 48	4 56	12 55	4 45	12 50	......

Extract from LT timetable, December 1935.

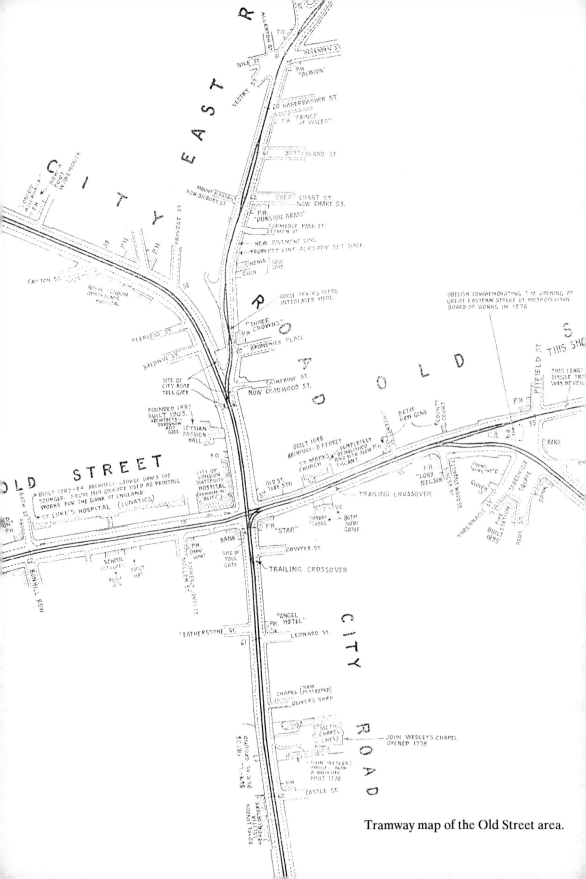

Tramway map of the Old Street area.

69. The twin trams and eccentric motorist have now fled the scene leaving a lone 31 at the red light. This is a convenient interchange point between trams and the tube trains which run through Old Street Station on the North-ern Line. In recent years this intersection has been completely redesigned to accommodate the increasing demands of the motor car. (H.B.Priestley)

70. We are now standing on the pavement outside Old Street Station. We note the disconnected east to south curves leading to Moorgate. Car 750 on service 43 continues along Old Street, whilst a trolleyless HR2 class car on service 11 has not long left the terminus and is now a few minutes into its half hour journey to Highgate Village. (H.Nicol)

71. Evening descends on Old Street at the corner of Pitfield Street. The cameraman will have to vacate the citybound track pronto as car 1959 accelerates towards him. Lengths of single track with double conduit existed at other places in London, but as a general rule most of the former LCC network was double track, and on Dog Kennel Hill quadruple track. (W.A.Camwell)

MOORGATE TO HIGHBURY CORNER

72. Moorgate was one of the LCC's most prestigious termini, but it still fell short of the real traffic objectives in the City. Nevertheless, many a city worker could enjoy a cup of coffee in Joe Lyons Corner House before catching the tram home. At peak times the speed of tram reversals was impressive, but at this midday the crew of car 548 have time to pose for a photograph. (W.A.Camwell)

73. Strictly speaking the terminus should be called Finsbury Pavement as the tracks ended in this thoroughfare at the corner of Ropemaker Street. The North Metropolitan horse car line opened on 7th May 1874; this postcard which is franked 3rd August 1904 shows some of the later, garden seat type of horse car. (D.Jones Coll.)

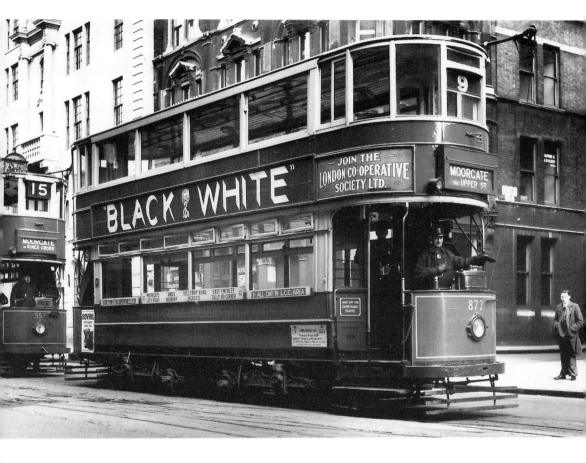

←————

74. Car 872 has arrived from Finchley whilst car 557 has done the trip from Parliament Hill Fields. On the rocker panel is the official Trolleybus for Trams notice. (W.A.Camwell)

←————

75. This tram advertises the Shilling (5p) All Day ticket which enabled Londoners to discover their town. This facility was also heavily used by tramway enthusiasts. Note the grab rails on the top deck ceiling of this service 15 car. (W.A.Camwell)

76. Service 83 passed into history on 5th February 1939 and the last ever tram to leave Moorgate departed on 10th December 1939. The section of track between Finsbury Square and Ropemaker Street was not replaced by trolleybuses. (H.Nicol)

77. So enthusiastic was the postcard publisher to join the twentieth century, that he produced this fake view of Finsbury Square. The horses pulling the tram have been painted out so as to give the impression that the area is now served by up-to-date electric cars. (J.H.Price Coll.)

78. Many a citizen has arrived in this world to the sound of tramcars passing outside the City of London Maternity Hospital seen on the left of the picture. Just north of here the tracks split and service 11 will diverge from City Road in the direction of East Road and New North Road. (H.B.Priestley)

79. We catch sight of car 521 in City Road near Shepherdess Walk. This vehicle is nearing the end of its working life and it will be scrapped rather than be moved over the water to a South London depot. Note the complete absence of traffic, a situation unimaginable in the congestion ridden 1990s. (H.B.Priestley)

80. This is the junction at New North Road Bridge which spans the Regent's Canal. This section of route was a late conversion to electric traction and horse cars operated until June 1913. The conversion was completed on 25th June 1914. The tracks to the left connect with Baring Street/New Street which opened on 26th November 1912 to replace the former horse tramway in Bridport Place and Mintern Street which was abandoned and removed. (D.Jones Coll.)

81. Number 41 was allocated in December 1912 to the tram service from Manor House to Baring Street. At the southern terminus we encounter car 1572 about to return to Manor House. (C.Carter Coll.)

ROUTE No. 7.

Moorgate to Highbury Station (via New North Road) and the Manor House, Finsbury Park

(Horse Traction).

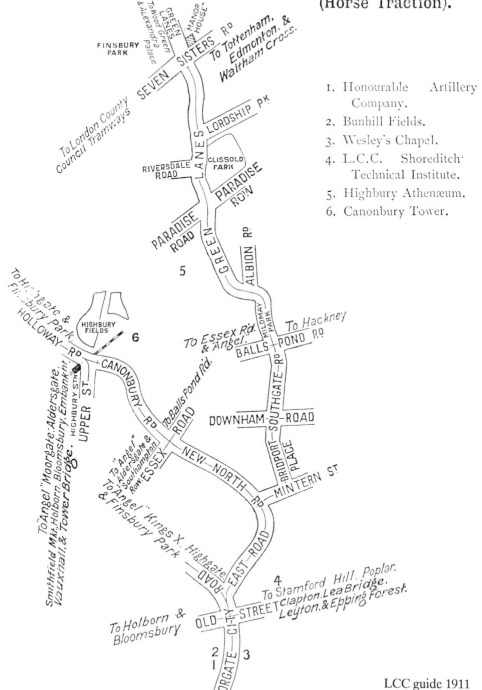

1. Honourable Artillery Company.
2. Bunhill Fields.
3. Wesley's Chapel.
4. L.C.C. Shoreditch Technical Institute.
5. Highbury Athenæum.
6. Canonbury Tower.

LCC guide 1911

82. At the corner of Southgate Road and Church Road a horse car pauses to pick up passengers outside the Jolly Farmers Inn. This horse tramway was opened on 7th May 1874 and closed on 11th December 1911 for reconstruction. This postcard view was sent in July 1905. (J.H.Price Coll.)

83. The spire of St.Stephens Church, Canonbury Road, appears to be rising from the roof of car 143 as it halts at the traffic lights. Note the curves in the foreground which lead into Essex Road. (H.B.Priestley)

84. At the top of Canonbury Road car 140 waits to swing into St. Paul's Road. The tell tale signs of trolleybus conversion are there for all to see and sister vehicle 143 will close service 11 on 10th December 1939. Seemingly the only person to see this tram on its final departure from Highgate Village was well known local enthusiast, John Barrie. Replacing trolleybus route 611 lasted until it in turn was replaced on 20th July 1960 by bus route 271. (H.B.Priestley)

Extract from LT timetable, December 1935.

		MON. to FRI.		SATURDAY		SUNDAY	
		First	Last	First	Last	First	Last
HIGHGATE VILLAGE — MOORGATE	Highgate Village to Moorgate	7 6	11 22	7 6 7 14	11 52	7 20	11 43
Via Highgate Hill, Holloway, Highbury, New North Road,	Highgate Village to Highgate (Archway Tav.)	7 6	11 58	7 6 7 14	12†32	7 20	12 24
East Road, City Road.　Through fare, 4d.	Moorgate to Highgate Village	7 4	11 27	7 3 7 15	12 0	7 54	11 54
Service Interval, 3—4 mins.　Journey time, 31 mins.	Moorgate to Highgate (Archway Tavern)	5 58 6 28	11 55	5 58 6 28	12 26	7 54	12 16
* Also 1239, 1 6, 132 to Highbury only.	Highgate (Archway Tav.) to Moorgate	5 30 6 0	11 28	5 30 6 0	11*53	7 26	11 49
† to Highbury.	Highgate (Archway Tav.) to Highgate Vill...	6 59	11 51	6 59	12 25	7 13	12 17

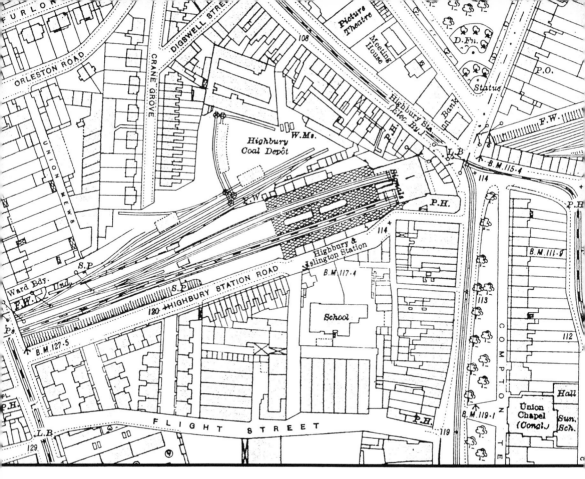

85. Even in Edwardian times Highbury Corner was a busy place as can be seen here with a range of public and private transport on display. The Holloway Road/Upper Street lines were electrified in 1906/07 and are fully described in *Hampstead and Highgate Tramways*. (J.H.Price Coll.)

86. Trams file past Highbury & Islington Station which was on the North London Railway. Much of this area was badly damaged during the bombing of the Second World War. (J.H.Price Coll.)

87. North of Highbury Corner services 11 and 35 once ran in tandem as far as Archway Tavern. Car 558, a class F Kingsway Subway car stands next to an M class tram which has just descended Highgate Hill. During the First World War the author's Great Aunt Grace worked as a conductress on a similar single deck car. The author himself has always had a liking for this class of tram, so maybe the answer lies in the genes! (H.Nicol)

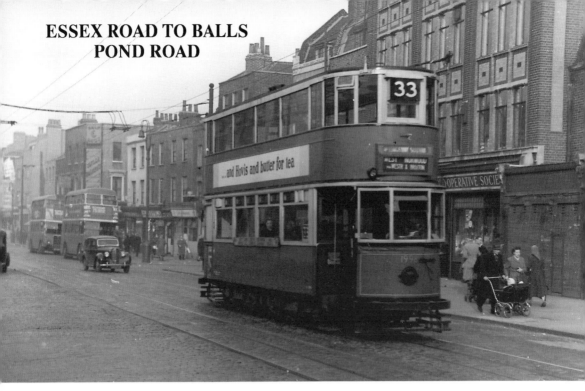

88. Service 33 provided the only railed transport along Essex Road after service 77 was replaced in September 1939. It survived the war and remained in splendid isolation fighting against competing trolleybuses and diesel buses until it succumbed to bus route 171 on 5th April 1952. Car 1998, depicted here near Britannia Row, worked from New Cross Depot during the final weeks of the system. (J.H.Meredith)

89. The Carlton Cinema by River Street forms the backdrop to this view of car 898 on service 77. This scene is just round the corner from picture 83. The motorman who is wearing his white topped summer hat, turns round to check all is clear before he moves forward to negotiate the points and crossings leading to Canonbury Road. (H.B.Priestley)

90. The photographer stands with his back to Essex Road tube station which was opened on 14th February 1904 as part of the Great Northern & City Railway. On the surface we notice a West Norwood bound 33 about to cross trolleybus route 611. (J.H.Price Coll.)

91. At the same spot as the previous photo, car 1993's progress has been halted by the lights. Much of the property hereabouts was "blitzed" in the war and St.Matthew's Church in the distance was left in ruins. (C.Carter)

92. Electric trams first appeared along Essex Road on 31st July 1909. Car 880 is seen working the Manor House to Aldersgate service which was later numbered 37. (J.H.Price Coll.)

93. A one way routeing for trams was instituted at the northern end of Essex Road. Here a 33 tram swings off Essex Road into Dove Road (formerly Dorset Street). (D.Jones Coll.)

94. We look east along Dove Road and note that this thoroughfare is also wired for trolleybuses, one of which can be seen in the far distance parked on the "wrong" side of the road. (H.B.Priestley)

95. The tracks in what was then Dorset Street were opened on 26th July 1913. This tram speeds away from the camera as we get a closer look at the elegant bowstring traction standards which carry the overhead used by short working trolleybuses. (C.Carter)

96. The face of Henry Brooke, the Conservative politician, glares out from an election poster on the corner of Dove Road and Southgate Road. On Thursday, 3rd April 1952 his party had more luck than the trams on service 33 which are now eking out their last hours. (R.J.Harley Coll.)

97. Car 1160 waits to make the left hand turn into Southgate Road in front of the rather aptly named Perseverance Tavern. (B.J.Cross Coll.)

98. Back on Essex Road there is an appreciable London Transport presence which includes car 2003 making its southbound journey to Bloomsbury and the Kingsway Subway. Notice that some of the trolleybus wiring from Essex Road into Dove Road has now been removed. (F.W.Ivey/LTPS)

100. This part of Balls Pond Road saw trams working in a westerly direction. Car 1940 has just emerged on to the double track at the corner of Essex Road. (C.Carter)

99. Continuing our wiring theme, we now encounter car 1907 which has developed plough trouble thus forcing it to use the trolleybus overhead. This practice was frowned upon by LT, but at times it was the only solution to get a disabled car out of the way. At any rate the tram crew look rather apprehensive as if they have been caught in the act...which they have, but we won't tell anybody! (D.A.Thompson)

Tramway map of the Balls Pond Road/Southgate Road area.

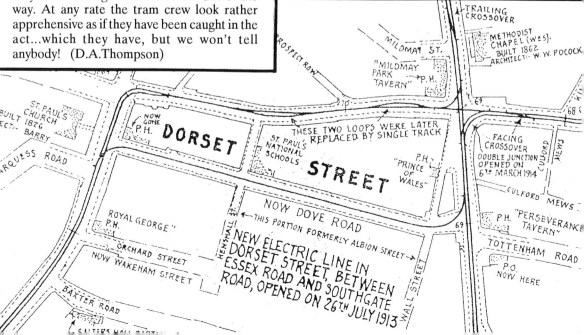

101. Car 176 leaves the single track in Balls Pond Road whilst on the opposite side a 677 trolleybus stops to pick up passengers. (F.W.Ivey/LTPS)

102. We finish our tour of North London at the corner of Mildmay Park and Balls Pond Road. A service 81 tram is about to cross the road junction and resume its journey towards Bloomsbury. The curves in the foreground lead into Southgate Road. (D.Jones Coll.)

ROLLING STOCK

WORKS CARS - Class L

Cars 011-012. These works cars were ordered by the LCC in 1909; they were designed as open vans with removable sides. Their main function was to transport wheelsets, traction motors and similar electrical items from Charlton Central Repair Depot (featured in Middleton Press volumes *Greenwich and Dartford Tramways* and *Eltham and Woolwich Tramways*) to other depots on the LCC network. Both trams were originally equipped with one trolley pole at each end of the car. The overhead equipment was of course additional to the standard conduit current collection apparatus. An unusual feature of each car was

the four wheel truck which was manufactured by Mountain and Gibson and included Warner radial components. The trolley poles were gradually removed from both vehicles leaving just the trolley standards - a view of car 012 in this condition is included in *Embankment and Waterloo Tramways* - thereby restricting these vehicles to conduit tracks only. The operational life of cars 011 and 012 was long and useful; they survived until the end of tramway operation in July 1952.

The plan of car 011 has been kindly supplied by Terry Russell. Other works cars will be featured in future albums.

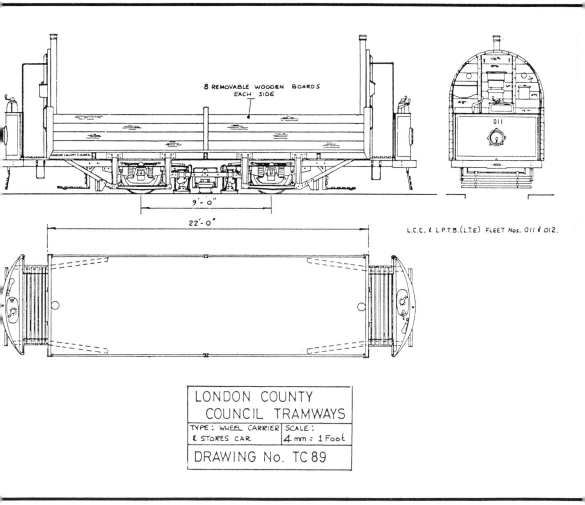

8 REMOVABLE WOODEN BOARDS EACH SIDE

011

9'- 0"

22'- 0"

L.C.C. & L.P.T.B.(L.T.E) FLEET Nos. 011 & 012.

LONDON COUNTY
COUNCIL TRAMWAYS

TYPE: WHEEL CARRIER & STORES CAR

SCALE: 4 mm = 1 Foot

DRAWING No. TC 89

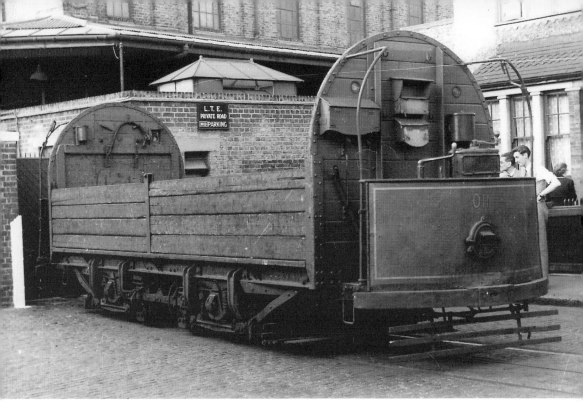

103. A group of enthusiasts gaze wistfully at car 011 which is positioned on the approach track to Charlton Works. The date is 5th July 1952 and this tram's working life is almost over. Tomorrow it will reside a short distance away at Penhall Road scrapyard. (J.H.Meredith)

104. We move back a few years to the 1930s when we catch sight of car 012 in Nelson Road, Greenwich. One wonders how far the motorman will have to pilot his charge - was it a local run as far as New Cross or a longer trek through the Kingsway Subway out to a depot on the north side? (H.Wightman)

105. Car 012 is pictured on 10th May 1952. This view shows the tram in final London Transport condition with the standard LT Gill Sans type of numeral. Note that the sides have been "unplanked" to reveal a full load of wheels and axles.   (J.C.Gillham)

106. Here we gain a detailed view of the Warner radial truck as car 012 stands outside the original entrance to New Cross Depot. (H.Wightman)

TRAM TOURS

The idea of viewing the capital's streets from the top deck of an omnibus seems to have become fashionable in Victorian days, however, the concept of running tram tours appears to have eluded the LCC and other metropolitan tramway operators. When the new owners took over in July 1933 the star of the tramcar began to wane; it was inconceivable that LT should actually promote a tourist attraction ride such as had been operated in Montreal and other cities around the world. After all, London was not a seaside resort like Southend or Blackpool, where special open cars catered for the trippers - the metropolis would have no truck with any tramway services beyond the mundane ones advertised in the timetable. Therefore, it must have come as a surprise to the decision makers at 55, Broadway when J.W.Fowler of the Light Railway Transport League proposed to charter car 1 for a jaunt from Waltham Cross to Purley - a trip across London from Hertfordshire to Surrey via the Kingsway Subway.

The attitude of London Transport to enthusiasts wishing to hire tour trams was always luke warm; this was in marked contrast to several provincial systems who went out of their way to accommodate the plans of visiting tramophiles. In the late 1940s and early 1950s as the replacement programme got going, the number of private tours increased, and the last one coincided appropriately with the final day of London's tramways.

107. Car 1 is seen on the memorable tour of 15th May 1938 when many enthusiasts realised a lifetime dream of crossing the capital in style from north to south. Along the route numerous photo stops were made and some of the precious cine film taken on this occasion has been included in a video tape by Online. This excursion was very timely as the pre-war trolleybus conversion scheme was soon to cut the mileage of North London's tramways drastically. (W.A.Camwell)

108. The social side of any tour was very important. Here on 3rd July 1949 we are faced by a group of the "enlightened ones" who are occupying the lower deck of car 1. In those days one had to have the courage of one's convictions to believe in the tramcar as the public transport vehicle of the future. It is sad that some of the people in this picture never lived to see the current British tramway revival. (J.H.Meredith)

109. One of the delights of touring was to use tracks where certain types of car would never have operated in scheduled service. Here, on Lewisham Road near the borough boundary dividing Greenwich and Lewisham, we observe car 1 on the single track and loops section over the old railway bridge which once crossed the defunct Greenwich Park branch. (J.H.Meredith)

LONDON TRAM TOUR.

5TH APRIL, 1952.

TOUR CARRIED OUT ON TWO 'LEYTON' E/3 CARS.

CAR 'A'   Nº 195   DRIVER - E.F. MILLS   CONDUCTOR - J. BISL

CAR 'B'   Nº 199   DRIVER - G.J. KENNARD   CONDUCTOR - J.D. DUF

MANOR HOUSE. 3·15

HIGHGATE. 2·35

START 2·30

Depot

REVERSE 2·50   ISLINGTON GREEN.

HOLBORN.

REVERSE 5·40   BLACKFRIARS.
sway Subway   CITY.

REVERSE 5·50

WESTMINSTER.

Kennington Brk Road {
No regular service since 7th April, 1951.

Charlton Works

Penhall Depot.

PASS 7·35

ABBEY W
Depot.

WOOLWICH.

KENNINGTON.

NEW CROSS.   GREENWICH.

Deptford P. Way Yard.
REVERSE 7·0

CAMBERWELL.   Depot   FINISH 8·0

LEWISHAM.

Car 'A'

BRIXTON.   LEE.   ELTHAM.

Car 'B'

Depot   6·45   FOREST HILL.

WEST NORWOOD.

TEA BREAK 4·15 - 5·0

110. On 5th April 1952 the LRTL hired two trams for a farewell tour of the Kingsway Subway services. As the accompanying map proves, it was nothing but thorough. Here at Manor House a solitary service 33 car is surrounded by camera toting enthusiasts determined to give the railbound vehicles a good send off.   (J.H.Meredith)

111. Trolleyless HR2 class car 120 can go no further along Downham Way as it has reached the end of the conduit track. As is customary on these occasions, the working of the change pit from overhead to conduit arouses a great deal of interest.   (J.H.Price)

112. On a Southern Counties Touring Society trip of 9th May 1948, a rehabilitated HR2 tram passes the Monkey Puzzle tree by the interlaced track on Brigstock Road, Thornton Heath. Local residents used to staid Croydon local service 42 would be unaccustomed to the sound of four-motor car 1885 which was decidedly overpowered for this tramway backwater. (A.J.Watkins Coll.)

113. A crew member switches the points for yet another circuit of the Festival of Britain roundabout on the eastern side of Westminster Bridge. Film buffs may recall, it was at this location that the pursuers of *Genevieve* came to grief on the tramlines in the famous British comedy production of 1952. (A.J.Watkins Coll.)

114. Car 1862 has now managed to emerge from Stangate into Westminster Bridge Road. From the look of things the rear platform seems to be overpopulated by a mixture of LT officials and enthusiasts. Above the fender the FAREWELL TOUR R.I.P. notice adds poignancy to the occasion. (J.H.Meredith)

56SP	L.C.C. TRAMWAYS	CC50.

7/-   **R.**

TO BE CANCELLED BELOW
DOUBLE LINE IF FARE CAN
BE REDUCED & REFUND IS
MADE

COMPLIMENTARY

1—Southampton Row	Waterloo Bridge—2 Savoy St.	**33**
2—Farringdon Road	Westminster Station—3	**35**
3—Angel	County Hall	
4—Cross St (Upper St) New North Rd.	York Road or—4 Christchurch	
5—Highbury Stn. or St. Paul's Rd. or Balls Pond Rd.	Elephant 5	
6—Holloway Rd. Stn. (Underground) or Albion Rd.	Camberwell Gate 6	
	Camberwell Green 7	
7—Nags Head or Lordship Pk	Town Hall 8 Camberwell	
8—Archway Tavern or Manor House	Rye Lane 9	
	Queens Rd Stn	
Holloway Stn., L.M.S.	New X Gate 10	
12—Norwood	Marquis of G'nby 11 or Malpas Rd (Lewisham High Road)	
11—Tulse Hill	Brockley Cross 12	
10—Herne Hill Stn or Croxted Rd.	Crofton Pk Stn 13	
9—George Canning or Dalberg Rd	Honor Oak Pk 14	
8—Brixton Stn (Acre Ln or Stockwell Rd)	Cranst'n Road 15	
7—Angell Road	Forest Hill Stn. 16	
6—Kennington Gate	Fitzalan Street 5	

(vertical text between columns:) Issued to commemorate closing of routes 33 and 35 5/4/52. Sub. way of Kingsway Sub. and abandonment of way

20SP	L.C.C. TRAMWAYS

ABBEY WOOD DEPOT

27—Abbey Wood	Ser.	City via Southwark	4
26—Basildon Rd (Junc. with McLeod Road).	**44**	St. George's Church	5
25—Wickham Lane	**46**	Tower Bridge Road	6
24—Plumstead Station	Ex.	Upper Grange Road	7
		Canal Bridge	8
23—Beresford Square		Old Kent Road Station	9
22—Nightingale Place		New Cross Gate	10
21—Prince Imperial Mon.		Marq. Granby or Malpas Rd (Lewisham High Road) or New X Stn (SECR)	11
20—Shooters Hill Road			
19—Well Hall Stn. or Admiral Seymour Road		Lewisham Rd Stn or Blackheath Rd. (Deptford Bridge)	12
18—Eltham High Street or Chapel St.		Lewisham Obelisk or King William St.	13
17—Middle Park Gates or Hardens Manor Way or Trinity St.		Glenton Rd or Blackwall Lane	14
16—Courtlands Avenue or Church Lane		Lee Road or Westcombe Hill	15

Ticket available without transfer on day of
issue only to stage point indicated by punch
hole. Issued subject to Council's by-laws, must
be shown or given up on demand.

Not transferable

SPECIAL TOUR
6th APRIL, 1952

115. New trackage, such as it was, acted as a magnet for enthusiast tours. Car 1877 precedes a service 70 tram on the temporary bridge which crosses Deptford Creek. This is an SCTS tour on 25th June 1950. (R.J.Harley Coll.)

116. A splendid setting for any special was on Lambeth Palace Road, outside the Archbishop of Canterbury's official residence. Whether the noble prelate was home, when car 1862 stopped outside on 22nd April 1951 is not recorded. (G.F.Ashwell)

Special tickets which were printed for tram tours have now become collectors' items. This reproduction of ticket 0050 for the April 1952 outing proves that seven shillings (35p) wisely spent will finance a journey lasting several hours where a liberal education on London's tramways will be provided in the company of like minded souls. Note the nostalgic harkback to the "great days" of the London County Council Tramways.

117. Car 1862 pauses for the photographer before the gentle ascent of Eltham Hill in the direction of Eltham Church. Flags and bunting can be seen attached to the car and the trolley rope. All this added to the occasion, and the scene is not lost on the rather tall lad with the school cap who has turned his head to observe this enthusiasts' special. (A.J.Watkins Coll.)

118. We now catch up with car 1908 on the final day of London's tramways, 5th July 1952. The location is Beresford Square, Woolwich on the connecting curve between the Eltham services and Beresford Street. In a few hours car 1908 will make its final journey to Penhall Road and oblivion. (J.H.Meredith)

FINALE

119. The end of the system is in sight and rather symbolically car 1960 finds itself positioned between its diesel bus and trolleybus rivals in Theobalds Road, Bloomsbury. London is emerging from the destruction of the Second World War and new streets and office buildings are part of a scenario which offers no role for the tramcar.
(A.J.Watkins Coll.)

120. As successors to the trams the trolleybuses worked in the area until they were replaced by diesel buses in 1959-61. This view presents an interesting comparison with picture 62; trolleybus route 677 was diverted to terminate at Smithfield rather than at Aldersgate, end of the line for tram service 77.
(C.Carter)

MP Middleton Press

Easebourne Lane, Midhurst. West Sussex. GU29 9AZ   Tel: 01730 813169   Fax: 01730 812601

..... *Write or telephone for our latest list* .....

BRANCH LINES
Branch Line to Allhallows
Branch Lines to Alton
Branch Lines around Ascot
Branch Line to Bude
Branch Lines around Canterbury
Branch Lines to East Grinstead
Branch Lines around Effingham Jn
Branch Lines to Exmouth
Branch Line to Fairford
Branch Lines to Hawkhurst
Branch Lines to Horsham
Branch Line to Ilfracombe
Branch Lines to Longmoor
Branch Line to Lyme Regis
Branch Line to Lynton
Branch Lines around Midhurst
Branch Line to Minehead
Branch Lines to Newport
Branch Line to Padstow
Branch Lines around Portmadoc 1923-46
Branch Lines around Porthmadog 1954-94
Branch Lines to Seaton & Sidmouth
Branch Line to Selsey
Branch Lines around Sheerness
Branch Line to Southwold
Branch Line to Swanage
Branch Line to Tenterden
Branch Lines to Torrington
Branch Lines to Tunbridge Wells
Branch Line to Upwell
Branch Lines around Weymouth

LONDON SUBURBAN RAILWAYS
Caterham and Tattenham Corner
Clapham Jn. to Beckenham Jn.
Crystal Palace and Catford Loop
Holborn Viaduct to Lewisham
Lines aound Wimbledon
London Bridge to Addiscombe
Mitcham Junction Lines
South London Line
West Croydon to Epsom
Willesden Junction to Richmond
Wimbledon to Epsom

STEAMING THROUGH
Steaming through Cornwall
Steaming through East Sussex
Steaming through the Isle of Wight
Steaming through Surrey
Steaming through West Hants
Steaming through West Sussex

GREAT RAILWAY ERAS
Ashford from Steam to Eurostar
Festiniog in the Fifties

COUNTRY BOOKS
Brickmaking in Sussex
East Grinstead Then and Now

SOUTH COAST RAILWAYS
Ashford to Dover
Bournemouth to Weymouth
Brighton to Eastbourne
Brighton to Worthing
Chichester to Portsmouth
Dover to Ramsgate
Hastings to Ashford
Ryde to Ventnor
Worthing to Chichester

SOUTHERN MAIN LINES
Bromley South to Rochester
Charing Cross to Orpington
Crawley to Littlehampton
Dartford to Sittingbourne
East Croydon to Three Bridges
Epsom to Horsham
Exeter to Barnstaple
Exeter to Tavistock
Faversham to Dover
Haywards Heath to Seaford
London Bridge to East Croydon
Orpington to Tonbridge
Sittingbourne to Ramsgate
Swanley to Ashford
Tonbridge to Hastings
Victoria to Bromley South
Waterloo to Windsor
Woking to Portsmouth
Woking to Southampton
Yeovil to Exeter

COUNTRY RAILWAY ROUTES
Andover to Southampton
Bath to Evercreech Junction
Bournemouth to Evercreech Jn
Burnham to Evercreech Junction
Croydon to East Grinstead
East Kent Light Railway
Fareham to Salisbury
Frome to Bristol
Guildford to Redhill
Porthmadog to Blaenau
Reading to Basingstoke
Reading to Guildford
Redhill to Ashford
Salisbury to Westbury
Strood to Paddock Wood
Taunton to Barnstaple
Westbury to Bath
Woking to Alton

TROLLEYBUS CLASSICS
Croydon's Trolleybuses
Woolwich & Dartford Trolleybuses

TRAMWAY CLASSICS
Aldgate & Stepney Tramways
Bournemouth & Poole Tramways
Brighton's Tramways
Bristol's Tramways
Camberwell & W. Norwood Tramways
Croydon's Tramways
Dover's Tramways
East Ham & West Ham Tramways
Eltham & Woolwich Tramways
Embankment & Waterloo Tramways
Exeter & Taunton Tramways
Greenwich & Dartford Tramways
Hampstead & Highgate Tramways
Hastings Tramways
Holborn & Finsbury Tramways
Ilford & Barking Tramways
Kingston & Wimbledon Tramways
Lewisham & Catford Tramways
Maidstone & Chatham Tramways
North Kent Tramways
Portsmouth's Tramways
Seaton & Eastbourne Tramways
Southampton Tramways
Southend-on-sea Tramways
Thanet's Tramways
Victoria & Lambeth Tramways
Walthamstow & Leyton Tramways
Wandsworth & Battersea Tramways

OTHER RAILWAY BOOKS
Garraway Father & Son
Industrial Railways of the South East
London Chatham & Dover Railway
South Eastern Railway
War on the Line

MILITARY BOOKS
Battle over Portsmouth
Battle Over Sussex 1940
Blitz Over Sussex 1941-42
Bognor at War
Bombers over Sussex 1943-45
Military Defence of West Sussex

WATERWAY ALBUMS
Hampshire Waterways
Kent and East Sussex Waterways
London to Portsmouth Waterway
West Sussex Waterways

BUS BOOK
Eastbourne Bus Story

SOUTHERN RAILWAY ● VIDEOS ●
Memories of the Hayling Island Branc
Memories of the Lyme Regis Branch
War on the Line

96